The God I Never Knew

Small Group Study Guide

Contents

How to Use
the Curriculum

1   This approach to group study has a simple design.
   Each week:

• **RECAP**
   Recap the previous week's session, inviting
   members to share about any opportunities they
   encountered throughout the week to apply what they
   learned (this doesn't apply to the first week).

• **THE ONE THING**
   This is a single statement that sums up the main point—
   the key idea—of the session.

• **ENGAGE**
   Ask the icebreaker question to help get people talking
   and feeling comfortable with one another.

• **WATCH**
   Watch the DVD. (If you don't have access to the
   companion DVD, read the short corresponding
   overview you'll find at the back of this study guide in
   the READ section.)

• **TALK**
   Discuss the questions.

• **PRAY**
   Pray together.

- **MEMORIZE**
  Encourage members to work on memorizing a key scripture verse.

- **EXPLORE**
  Encourage members to complete the journal portion before the next meeting.

2 Generate participation and discussion. Resist the urge to teach. Ask open-ended questions—questions that can't be answered with "yes" or "no" (e.g., "What do you think about that?" rather than "Do you agree?"). When a question does arise, ask the group for their input instead of answering it yourself right off the bat. Be comfortable with silence. If you ask a question and no one responds, rephrase the question and wait for a response. Remember, your primary role is to create an environment where people feel comfortable to be themselves and participate, not to provide the answers to all of their questions.

3 Ask the group to pray for each other from week to week, especially about key issues that arise during your group time. This is how you begin to build authentic community and encourage spiritual growth within the group.

KEYS TO A DYNAMIC SMALL GROUP

Relationships
Meaningful, encouraging relationships are the foundation of a dynamic small group. Teaching, discussion, worship and prayer are important elements of a group meeting, but the depth of each element is often dependent upon the depth of the relationships between members.

Availability
Building a sense of community within your group requires members to prioritize their relationships with one another. This means being available to listen, care for one another and meet each other's needs.

Mutual Respect
Mutual respect is shown when members value others' opinions (even when they disagree) and are careful to never belittle or embarrass others in the group (including their spouses, who may or may not be present).

Openness
A healthy small group environment encourages sincerity and transparency. Members treat each other with grace in areas of weakness, allowing each other room to grow.

Confidentiality
To develop authenticity and a sense of safety within the group, each member must be able to trust that things discussed within the group will not be shared outside the group.

Shared Responsibility
Group members will share the responsibility of group meetings by using their God-given abilities to serve at each gathering. Some may greet, some may host, some may teach,

etc. Ideally, each person should be available to care for one another as needed.

Sensitivity
Dynamic small groups are born when the leader consistently seeks and is responsive to the guidance of the Holy Spirit, following His leading throughout the meeting as opposed to sticking to the "agenda." This is especially important during the discussion and ministry time.

Fun!
Dynamic small groups take the time to have fun! Create an atmosphere for fun, and be willing to laugh at yourselves every now and then!

Discovering a God I Never Knew

One Thing

The Holy Spirit is not an "it." He is a full, co-equal member of the Godhead. As such, He is a "person" with all the attributes of personhood, including a soul. That means we have the opportunity to have a real, transformative relationship with Him.

Engage

Do you have a favorite old T-shirt?
Pair of sneakers?
Cereal bowl?

To what inanimate object in your life are you most attached?

Watch

Watch Robert Morris' teaching titled "Discovering a God I Never Knew."* As you view it:

• **Look for the three elements that make up a "soul."**

• **Listen for a vital key to discovering God's will for your life in every situation.**

*(If you are not able to watch this teaching on DVD or for additional study on this topic, turn to the Week 1 Notes on page 72 in the "Read" section.)

Talk

For group discussion or personal reflection:

QUESTION 1

If you grew up in church, how was the topic of the Holy Spirit handled where you attended? If you didn't attend church, what was your concept of the Holy Spirit (or "Holy Ghost" in some circles)?

QUESTION 2

Why is it so important to understand that the Holy Spirit is a person? How would someone relate to the Holy Spirit differently when they view Him as a person and not a "force?"

QUESTION 3

Have you ever felt reluctant to open yourself to the Holy Spirit's influence because you feared it would result in your appearing strange or odd to others? What, specifically, were you afraid of?

QUESTION 4

Read Galatians 5:22-23. What does this list of the "fruits of the Spirit" reveal to you about the Holy Spirit's personality and temperament? How does this picture compare with the way you have perceived the Holy Spirit in the past?

QUESTION 5

Read John 16:12-15. One of the Holy Spirit's roles is to guide you into all truth. In what area(s) of your life do you have key questions or consistent confusion? What would you like the Holy Spirit to reveal to you?

Pray

Take some time as a group to lift one another up in the light of the truths discussed in this session.

Explore

Want to go deeper? Here is some food for thought, prayer, and journaling in the coming week.

KEY QUOTE:

"You have someone living inside of you who knows everything about everything. And He has committed Himself to be your teacher and to lead you into all truth."

–Robert Morris

Write a note to God the Holy Spirit expressing a desire to get to know Him better as a person.

Dear Holy Spirit,

_____

_____

_____

_____

However, when He, the Spirit of truth, has come, He will guide you into all truth; for He will not speak on His own authority, but whatever He hears He will speak; and He will tell you things to come. (John 16:13)

What kinds of things do you need the Spirit to teach you?
What kinds of truth do you need Him to lead you into?

_____

_____

_____

_____

KEY VERSES:
John 16:13
Galatians 5:22–23
Ephesians 4:25–32

What stands out to you as you read these verses?

_____

_____

_____

_____

What is the Holy Spirit saying to you through these scriptures?

_____

_____

_____

_____

KEY QUESTION:
Ask the Holy Spirit, "Is there any practice, habit or other sin in my life that grieves you?" Listen for an answer and write down what you hear Him saying to you:

_____

_____

_____

_____

KEY PRAYER:
Holy Spirit, please forgive me if I've ever viewed you as an impersonal thing or "it." And I'm sorry for the times I've "stiff-armed" you when all you wanted was to help, protect and guide me. Today I want to start a new chapter in our relationship. Help me get to know you as you truly are.

What is This Person Like?

Recap

In the previous section, we discussed that the Holy Spirit is a person, and we can have a personal relationship with Him. In the past week, have you been more aware of His presence? If so, how did that awareness change your thoughts, actions or experiences?

One Thing

Helper. Friend. God. The Holy Spirit isn't strange. He is a wonderful, kind, and sensitive person. And real friendship with Him will change your life.

Engage

There are a lot of odd people in the world. What's the goofiest thing you've ever seen someone do in public?

Watch

Watch Robert Morris' teaching titled "What is This Person Like?"* As you view it:

- **Look for three key things about which the Holy Spirit comes to "convince" us.**

- **Watch for the three facets of the Holy Spirit's role and personality.**

*(If you are not able to watch this teaching on DVD or for additional study on this topic, turn to the Week 2 Notes on page 77 in the "Read" section.)

Talk

For group discussion or personal reflection:

QUESTION 1

In your life thus far, has "The Comforter" (the Holy Spirit) been for "daily use," or "for looks only?"

QUESTION 2

The name "Helper" is translated from the Greek word parakletos meaning comforter, intercessor, consoler, and advocate. Which of these descriptions of the Holy Spirit's work has the most significance to you personally? Why?

QUESTION 3

Have you ever experienced supernatural "help" that you knew came from The Helper—the Holy Spirit? Describe your experience.

QUESTION 4

Read John 16:8–10. One of the Holy Spirit's roles is to convict, or convince, us of these truths. How had you understood "conviction" before now? What do you understand about the heart behind the Holy Spirit's conviction now?

QUESTION 5

In your own words, describe what the Holy Spirit is like.

Pray

Take some time as a group to lift one another up in the light of the truths discussed in this session.

Explore

Want to go deeper? Here is some food for thought, prayer, and journaling in the coming week.

KEY QUOTE:

"The evidence of the Holy Spirit's presence in your life is not one particular gift. It is all the gifts. It's also the fruit and the power and the love of God poured out through His people."

–Robert Morris

What evidence can I point to of the Holy Spirit's presence in my life?

Describe any fears or apprehensions you may have had in the past about allowing the Holy Spirit's full freedom to work in you and through you:

KEY VERSES:
John 14:16, 25, 26
John 16:12–15

What stands out to you as you read these verses?

_____

_____

_____

_____

What is the Holy Spirit saying to you through these scriptures?

_____

_____

_____

_____

KEY QUESTION:
What are some areas of consistent struggle, defeat or confusion in which you could use a Helper?

_____

_____

_____

_____

KEY PRAYER:
Holy Spirit, thank you for your ministry of help, comfort, direction and revelation in my life. Please show me any barriers or walls I've put up that keep me from receiving all the wonderful benefits of that ministry. I welcome your presence and work in my life today.

The Grand Entry

Recap

In the previous section, we learned that one key descriptive name of the Holy Spirit is "the Helper." Were there any instances this last week in which you received special help from Him?

One Thing

The outpouring of the Holy Spirit on the Day of Pentecost was one of the most significant events in human history. It's an event that is as relevant today as it was 2,000 years ago.

Engage

Israel had three major annual feasts and seven total. What is your favorite holiday and why?

Watch

Watch Robert Morris' teaching titled "The Grand Entry."*
As you view it:

- **Look for the two distinct but related "language" miracles that followed the outpouring of the Holy Spirit.**

- **Note which Genesis event is paralleled (in reverse) by the Day of Pentecost.**

*(If you are not able to watch this teaching on DVD or for additional study on this topic, turn to the Week 3 Notes on page 81 in the "Read" section.)

Talk

For group discussion or personal reflection:

QUESTION 1
What is the most unusual thing you have ever witnessed in a large crowd of people?

QUESTION 2

The giving of the Holy Spirit was a supernaturally unifying event. Is there an area of your life—family, work, or school—in which greater unity is needed? How might the fruit or power of the Holy Spirit make a difference in this situation?

QUESTION 3

Read Acts 2:41-47. According to this passage, how was the infilling of the Holy Spirit reflected in the actions and attitudes of the believers after the Day of Pentecost?

QUESTION 4

It's easy to see the evidence of the Holy Spirit's presence in the lives of others, but we're often blind to His work and power in ourselves. Point out some ways you have observed the Holy Spirit's activity in the life of another person in the group. (If you don't know any other group members well, talk about the evidence of His work in another person you know.)

Pray

Take some time as a group to lift one another up in the light of the truths discussed in this session.

Explore

Want to go deeper? Here is some food for thought, prayer, and journaling in the coming week.

KEY QUOTE:

"The Holy Spirit gives us the power to live righteously in an unrighteous world. I don't want to ever go back to simply being a Christian and wanting to do the right thing but not having the power to do it."

–Robert Morris

Is there a gap between the Christian life you desire to live and the one you're currently living? Describe any areas of frustration and consistent falling short.

Romans 8:1-9 speaks of "walking according to the Spirit" and having a mind "set on the Spirit." What do you think this looks like in daily, real-world practice?

KEY VERSES:
Acts 1:4–5
Acts 2:1–13; 37–39
Romans 8:1–9
Ephesians 5:18

What stands out to you as you read these verses?

What is the Holy Spirit saying to you through these scriptures?

KEY QUESTION:
On Mount Sinai, God expressed His will on tablets of stone. On the Day of Pentecost, He sent His Spirit to write His will and Word upon the human heart. In this quiet moment, ask the Holy Spirit to write upon your own heart. Take some time to be still and listen, then write what you hear Him saying to you:

_____

_____

_____

KEY PRAYER:
Father, I want to experience the fulfillment of the Feast of Pentecost in my life. Holy Spirit, I receive you into my life. I welcome you with an open heart. I ask you to fill me, from top to bottom; to the core of who I am; with your power, your love, your gifts, and your peace, so I can abundantly bear your fruit.

The Power Transfer

Recap

In the previous section we learned that God chose the Day of Pentecost—a Jewish festival commemorating His writing the law upon stone on Mt. Sinai—to pour out the Holy Spirit in a new way into the hearts of His people. Were there any occasions this past week in which you were aware of the Holy Spirit writing God's will or wishes upon your heart?

One Thing

The New Testament clearly speaks of three baptisms—one we can witness with our natural eyes and two that are spiritual in nature.

Engage

What's the longest period of time you've ever had to live without electricity? What creative things did you have to do to manage?

_____

_____

_____

_____

Watch

Watch Robert Morris' teaching titled "The Power Transfer."*
As you view it:

- Take note of "who" is doing the baptizing in each of the three baptisms mentioned.

- Look for the surprising and little-known "last words of Jesus."

*(If you are not able to watch this teaching on DVD or for additional study on this topic, turn to the Week 4 Notes on page 85 in the "Read" section.)

Talk

For group discussion or personal reflection:

QUESTION 1

Hebrews 6:1-3 speaks of moving on to maturity from a foundation of "elementary" things. What do you consider to be the marks and characteristics of a "mature" believer?

QUESTION 2

Were you ever baptized in water? If so, what was your understanding of what was taking place spiritually?

QUESTION 3

Jesus instructed his followers to stay in Jerusalem and "wait for the Promise of the Father" (meaning the Holy Spirit). How good are you at *waiting*? Describe a time in which you've experienced a season of waiting for a promise of God.

QUESTION 4

Submitting to water baptism requires a certain level of trust in the baptizer (you surrender control of your body to another person and allow him to submerge you—trusting him to bring you back up!). Allowing Jesus to baptize us in the Holy Spirit also requires a level of trust. In what ways has Jesus demonstrated His trustworthiness in your life? What do you believe He is showing you about the Holy Spirit today?

Pray

Take some time as a group to lift one another up in the light of the truths discussed in this session.

Explore

Want to go deeper? Here is some food for thought, prayer, and journaling in the coming week.

KEY QUOTE:

"When I get saved, I become a new creation. When I get water baptized, the old person—the flesh—is cut off. When I get baptized in the Holy Spirit, I get the power to walk in the new."
                                                                    –Robert Morris

Write down the dates on which you believe you received each of the three baptisms mentioned in this section. (If you have not yet received one or more of these, or aren't sure, leave that part blank.)

I was baptized into Jesus (Salvation) on:

Date: _____

I was baptized in water on:

Date: _____

I was baptized in the Holy Spirit on:

Date: _____

Write down any outstanding memories, thoughts or feelings surrounding these events.

_____

_____

_____

_____

KEY VERSES:
Hebrews 6:1–3
Matthew 3:11
Acts 1:4–5, 8
1 John 5:7–8

What stands out to you as you read these verses?

_____

_____

_____

_____

What is the Holy Spirit saying to you through these scriptures?

_____

_____

_____

_____

KEY QUESTION:
Read Romans 7:15–25. Here, Paul describes the frustration of trying to live the Christian life in his own strength. Can you identify with Paul's "wretched" feeling of frustration? Express that inward battle in words:

Now read Romans 8:1–9. Paul presents the answer to this dilemma as "living according to the Spirit." Write a prayer submitting to the Holy Spirit's help in learning to walk "according to the Spirit."

KEY PRAYER:
Thank you for salvation. Thank you for the wonderful outward symbol and inward work of water baptism. And Jesus, I thank you for your desire to baptize me in the amazing person of the Holy Spirit, just as you were. Lord, I trust you. Help me trust you more. Forgive me for any patterns of thought or action that have been resistant to your highest and best will for me.

Power for Living a Supernatural Life

Recap

In the previous session, we discovered that a "third baptism"—Jesus baptizing us in the Holy Spirit—is the source of supernatural power to live the Christian life. Were you aware of any moments in the previous week in which you needed or received divine help?

One Thing

There are three baptisms and three "witnesses" which testify of the full, redemptive work God wants to do in the life of every person. The Old Testament is rich with symbolism pointing us to baptism in the Holy Spirit as the key to a Christian life characterized by supernatural power.

Engage

It seems every comic book superhero has come to life in a Hollywood movie in recent years. If you could possess one "superpower," what would it be?

Watch

Watch Robert Morris' teaching titled "Power for Living a Supernatural Life."* As you view it:

- **Look for the symbolism of three baptisms in Abraham's life.**
- **Watch for the hidden symbolism of the blood applied to the doorposts at the first Passover.**

*(If you are not able to watch this teaching on DVD or for additional study on this topic, turn to the Week 5 Notes on page 89 in the "Read" section.)

Talk

For group discussion or personal reflection:

QUESTION 1

Paul asked the new Christians of Ephesus if they had "received the Holy Spirit since they believed." Their response was, "We have not so much as heard whether there is a Holy Spirit." How much teaching about the Holy Spirit did you receive immediately after being born again? What were you told?

QUESTION 2

Acts 8 and Acts 19 tell of believers who were recently saved and water baptized being invited by Jesus' disciples to receive the Holy Spirit as well. At any point in your Christian life, have you had the sense that you were "missing something?" Why? Describe that feeling.

QUESTION 3

God changed the names of Abram and Sarai after He entered into covenant with them. In changing Sarai to Sarah, God "took the 'I' out and put the Spirit in." In what area of your life would it be good to have less "I" and more Holy Spirit?

QUESTION 4

In the wilderness, a cloud led the children of Israel by day and pillar of fire by night. The Holy Spirit wants to lead us today, but through different means. In what ways have you experienced His guidance?

Pray

Take some time as a group to lift one another up in the light of the truths discussed in this session.

Explore

Want to go deeper? Here is some food for thought, prayer, and journaling in the coming week.

KEY QUOTE:

"How many times in your Christian walk have you known you needed supernatural power? That's all of us isn't it? Well, that is why Jesus sent the Holy Spirit."

–Robert Morris

Write a list of the various life-roles you fulfill each week (e.g. wife/husband, mother/father, employee, volunteer, caregiver, etc.).

My Roles

1. _____

2. _____

3. _____

4. _____

5. _____

6. _____

7. _____

For each role, write down some ways you would benefit from supernatural help.

1. _____

2. _____

3. _____

4. _____

5. _____

6. _____

7. _____

KEY VERSES:
Genesis 15:17–18
1 Corinthians 10:1–11
Colossians 1:13

What stands out to you as you read these verses?

_____

_____

_____

_____

What is the Holy Spirit saying to you through these scriptures?

_____

_____

_____

_____

KEY QUESTION:
Have you received a "third baptism?" If not, are there any questions or concerns keeping you from freely and confidently asking Jesus to baptize you in the Holy Spirit right now? If yes, what?

_____

_____

_____

_____

KEY PRAYER:
(If you want to experience that right now, return to the end of this week's video segment and join in the group prayer to receive the baptism in the Holy Spirit.) Or pray . . .

Father, I thank you for sending the gift of the Holy Spirit. I ask you to fill me with Your Holy Spirit right now. Baptize me from the top of my head to the bottom of my feet with your precious Holy Spirit. I receive You, Holy Spirit, by faith, fully and completely. In Jesus' name . . .

The Bringer of Gifts

Recap

In the previous section, we saw that baptism in the Holy Spirit was repeatedly foreshadowed in the Old Testament and encouraged by leaders of the early Church. With it comes supernatural assistance and power to live the Christian life. Did you partake of that power in the past week? If so, how?

One Thing

God didn't send the Holy Spirit to us empty handed. Not only is His role and title "Helper," He brings divine gifts to anyone who opens his or her heart to His supernatural help. Together, they provide the Spirit-filled, Spirit-yielded believer with an amazing array of supernatural ways to bless others.

Engage

What is the most meaningful or memorable gift you have ever received from another person?

Watch

Watch Robert Morris' teaching titled "The Bringer of Gifts."*
As you view it:

• **Listen for the three categories of divine gifts.**

• **Watch for the remarkable story about "Mr. America."**

*(If you are not able to watch this teaching on DVD or for additional study on this topic, turn to the Week 6 Notes on page 95 in the "Read" section.)

Talk

For group discussion or personal reflection:

QUESTION 1

What first comes to mind when you hear the terms charisma and charismatic? What connotations do you associate with each word?

QUESTION 2

1 Corinthians 12:7 says, "But the manifestation of the Spirit is given to each one for the profit of all." In what ways have you been aware of the Holy Spirit working through you to the profit of those around you?

QUESTION 3

A word of knowledge is "to know something specific without having learned it by natural means." Have you ever received a word of knowledge from another believer? If you are comfortable talking about it, describe the experience.

QUESTION 4

A word of wisdom is "a divine answer or solution for a particular situation." It often involves supernatural knowledge of what to *say* or *do* in challenging circumstances. Describe a past situation in which it would have made a big difference to have had supernatural wisdom.

Pray

Take some time as a group to lift one another up in the light of the truths discussed in this session.

Explore

Want to go deeper? Here is some food for thought, prayer, and journaling in the coming week.

KEY QUOTE:

"You can have any and all of the [nine] gifts as the Holy Spirit wills, [He] distributes them when you need them. But the gifts belong to Him. Here's the gift we have—the gift of the Holy Spirit's presence in our lives."

–Robert Morris

Write a thank you note to God for the gift of the Holy Spirit:

As you heard descriptions of the three gifts defined in this session (word of knowledge, discerning of spirits, and word of wisdom) what emotions or thoughts did you have when you imagined yourself operating in these at a higher level?

What steps can you take to be more sensitive to opportunities to express these gifts and yield to the Holy Spirit's nudges and promptings?

KEY VERSES:
1 Corinthians 12:1–11

What stands out to you as you read these verses?

What is the Holy Spirit saying to you through these scriptures?

KEY QUESTION:

Have you ever had someone refuse a gift you were trying to give them? Describe your feelings:

KEY PRAYER:

Father, as I go about my days, help me be more sensitive and aware of the gift of the Holy Spirit within. Grant me both the ability to hear the promptings of the Spirit and the courage to act on them.

More Gifts

Recap

In the previous section, we examined the first category of gifts—the Discerning Gifts. Did you notice these gifts in operation this past week in yourself or in others?

One Thing

The nine gifts of the Spirit listed in 1 Corinthians 12 can be grouped into three categories—Discerning Gifts, Declarative Gifts, and Dynamic Gifts. The Declarative Gifts involve using the spoken word to bless, encourage and strengthen others. The Dynamic Gifts involve expressions of God's miraculous power.

Engage

If you could take a pill and be instantly fluent in a foreign language, what language would you learn and why?

Watch

Watch Robert Morris' teaching titled "More Gifts."*
As you view it:

- **Watch for the three effects the genuine gift of prophecy will always have on the hearer.**

- **Look for the reason Paul referred to "gifts of healings" (plural) rather than gifts of "healing" (singular)."**

*(If you are not able to watch this teaching on DVD or for additional study on this topic, turn to the Week 7 Notes on page 100 in the "Read" section.)

Talk

For group discussion or personal reflection:

QUESTION 1
Have you felt that God wanted you to tell someone something, but you didn't do it? What kept you from speaking out?

_____

_____

_____

_____

QUESTION 2

All believers are encouraged to have faith. However, the "gift of faith" is a grant of supernatural confidence or peace in extraordinary circumstances. Have you or someone you know ever experienced this gift? Describe the event.

QUESTION 3

Testimonies of miracles seem to be much more common in Third World countries than in the most developed nations such as the U.S. and Europe. Give some reasons why you think this is the case.

QUESTION 4

In practical terms, what do you think it means to say "hello" to the Holy Spirit?

Pray

Take some time as a group to lift one another up in the light of the truths discussed in this session.

Explore

Want to go deeper? Here is some food for thought, prayer, and journaling in the coming week.

KEY QUOTE:

"All of these gifts have to do with ministry to people. They are all about encouraging people. God is an encourager, not a discourager."

–Robert Morris

1 Corinthians 14:31 says, "You can all prophesy . . ." Ask the Holy Spirit to give you a prophetic word of encouragement for someone you know. Write down what you hear Him saying:

Are you in need of some encouragement right now? Describe the source or area of your discouragement.

Now ask the Holy Spirit to speak to you about this area. Ask Him to show you the Father's perspective of the situation. Write down any impressions or truths that come to your mind.

KEY VERSES:
1 Corinthians 12:1-11
1 Corinthians 14:1-3
1 Corinthians 14:39

What stands out to you as you read these verses?

What is the Holy Spirit saying to you through these scriptures?

KEY QUESTION:
Paul spends a significant percentage of the 12th and 14th chapters of 1 Corinthians providing guidance on the use of the gifts of the Spirit. In between these we find "the love chapter"—chapter 13. What message do you take away from that fact?

KEY PRAYER:
Hello, Holy Spirit, what do You want to do with me, in me, and through me today? I welcome your presence with me. I embrace the gifts you want to manifest in me. I yield to your desire to strengthen, encourage and bless others through me. Let's do amazing things together.

The Language of Heaven

Recap

In the previous section, we explored the Declarative and Dynamic Gifts. In what ways did a fresh awareness and deeper understanding of these gifts impact your week?

One Thing

The grace of prayer language (praying or singing in tongues) is a beautiful and beneficial gift from God. It enables the believer to pray-out truths beyond his or her human understanding while building themselves up in faith and spiritual strength.

Engage

Exercise is obviously a great way to build up your physical strength. What is your favorite form of exercise? And your least favorite?

Watch

Watch Robert Morris' teaching titled "The Language of Heaven."* As you view it:

- **Look for Robert Morris' personal account of struggling to release his prayer language and what triggered his breakthrough.**
- **Watch for the surprising promise Jesus made that should reassure every person who is seeking to be more open to the Holy Spirit's influence.**

*(If you are not able to watch this teaching on DVD or for additional study on this topic, turn to the Week 8 Notes on page 104 in the "Read" section.)

Talk

For group discussion or personal reflection:

QUESTION 1

Have you ever witnessed what you would describe as a true "revival" or a "move of God?" Describe it.

_____

_____

_____

_____

QUESTION 2

Romans 8:26 says, "Likewise the Spirit also helps in our weaknesses. For we do not know what we should pray for as we ought, but the Spirit Himself makes intercession for us with groanings which cannot be uttered" (NKJV). Have you ever faced a problem so mystifying that you didn't even know how to begin praying about it? What did you do? How did you pray?

QUESTION 3

When you pray in tongues, your "spirit prays" (1 Corinthians 14:14); you strengthen yourself spiritually (1 Corinthians 14:4, Jude 20); and it constitutes a key part of the "whole armor of God" (Ephesians 6:11). Why do you think praying in the Spirit is such a powerful and versatile act?

QUESTION 4

You have heard and discussed who the Holy Spirit is, what He is like, and what He does. Now, what would you like the Holy Spirit to do in and through your life?

_____

_____

_____

_____

QUESTION 5

The baptism in the Holy Spirit is scriptural, it's beneficial, and it's a choice. Would you like to be baptized in the Holy Spirit? If so, ask Jesus to baptize you in the Holy Spirit today.

_____

_____

_____

_____

Pray

Take some time as a group to lift one another up in the light of the truths discussed in this session.

Explore

Want to go deeper? Here is some food for thought, prayer, and journaling in the coming week.

KEY QUOTE:

"Praying 'in the Spirit' in unknown tongues. It's biblical. It's a benefit. And it's a choice."

–Robert Morris

Read each of the following scriptures in your own Bible and summarize in your own words the benefit of praying in the Spirit promised by the passage:

1 Corinthians 14:4

Benefit: _____

Ephesians 6:10–18

Benefit: _____

Romans 8:26,27

Benefit: _____

Jude v. 20

Benefit: _____

Once you have received the baptism in the Holy Spirit, releasing the gift of praying in tongues is a choice, i.e., a voluntary act of your will. Describe what, if anything, is keeping you from stepping out and speaking out?

_____

_____

_____

Pray for help in overcoming the hindrances described above then speak out in syllables or phrases that rise up in your awareness. Describe what happened:

_____

_____

_____

KEY VERSES:
Acts 10:44-48
1 Corinthians 12:1-11, 14:1-19

What stands out to you as you read these verses?

_____

_____

_____

_____

What is the Holy Spirit saying to you through these scriptures?

_____

_____

_____

_____

KEY QUESTION:

"How much more will your heavenly Father give the Holy Spirit to those who ask Him!" (Luke 11:13). Write a prayer, asking the Father for a fresh filling of the Holy Spirit and for greater grace to yield to Him:

_____

_____

_____

_____

KEY PRAYER:

Father, thank you for the Helper—God, the Holy Spirit—living and working in me. I welcome His presence. I embrace His gifts. I respond to His promptings and direction. I allow Him to pray through me because He knows your will much better than I do. And I allow Him to give voice to my worship because He can communicate things I don't have words to express.

Read

Week 1

Discovering a God I Never Knew

Do you have a favorite chair? If so, you may really love it. But it doesn't love you back. In fact, you can't have a relationship with it at all.

Notice that in the sentences above, the chair is an "it." Most of us learned in our earliest English classes that the pronoun "it" refers to something that isn't a person. Yet people frequently use this pronoun when speaking of the Holy Spirit.

This kind of language reveals a mindset that the Holy Spirit isn't a person but rather some sort of impersonal force.

This view presents a big problem. If you don't see the Holy Spirit as a person, you'll never develop a personal relationship with Him. Why? Because, you don't develop a personal relationship with a thing or a force.

We can only experience the amazing benefits and joys that come with a friendship with the Holy Spirit when we fully understand that He is a person.

How can we know for sure He is a person? Well, how do we know anyone is a person? What constitutes personhood? Some people might say, "A person has life." Well, a tree has life, too. Nevertheless, a tree isn't a person. A person is a being with a soul.

The idea that God has a soul can seem a little strange. However, Scripture tells us that He does. In Matthew 12:18,

God the Father speaks and says of Jesus, "Behold my servant, whom I have chosen, my beloved in whom my soul is well pleased." That's pretty clear!

So what about the Holy Spirit? In Hebrews 10:38, the Spirit of God declares, "Now the just shall live by faith, if anyone draws back, my soul has no pleasure in him."

God the Father, God the Son, and God the Holy Spirit all have souls, and all fit the definition of personhood. The Bible says the soul is comprised of our mind, will and emotions. The Holy Spirit has thoughts, a will and emotions like the rest of the Godhead.

What is the mind of the Holy Spirit like? He is God! You have someone living inside you who knows everything about everything, and He has committed Himself to be your teacher and lead you into all truth!

More than anything else, Christians struggle and long to know God's will for their lives. In fact, surveys reveal that the number one spiritual question believers ask is, "How can I know the will of God?" The answer is to know the Holy Spirit.

You have someone living in you who knows the will of God for your life. If you want to get to know the will of God, get to know the Holy Spirit. Your friendship with Him can truly change your life. Friendship with the Holy Spirit is possible because He is a person.

You can't have a personal relationship with someone through someone else. God wants to talk to you personally, and He will do it through the Holy Spirit.

Like any other person with a soul, the Holy Spirit also has emotions. Look at the list of "the fruit of the Spirit." These are the attributes of a person. Indeed, these traits arise in anyone who allows the Holy Spirit to express Himself in his or her life.

The fruit of the Spirit is love, joy, peace, longsuffering, kindness, goodness, faithfulness, gentleness, and self-control (See Galatians 5:22–23).

A chair can't love. It will never experience joy. Only a person can experience peace. The same goes for kindness, goodness, faithfulness, gentleness, and self-control. These are characteristics of a person.

In the same way, only a person can feel the opposite of joy—grief. In Ephesians 4:30 we read this warning: "And do not grieve the Holy Spirit of God, by whom you were sealed for the day of redemption."

So just what is grief? Grief is simply sadness you feel at the loss of connection with someone. We traditionally associate grief with the death of someone we love, because death creates a break in fellowship with the person who dies. But our hurtful thoughts and actions can also cause a temporary loss of fellowship. So we must ask ourselves a key question: What grieves the Holy Spirit?

Obviously, sin does, but not for the reason most people assume.

Sin doesn't grieve the Holy Spirit because He's a prude and doesn't want you to have fun. Sin grieves the Holy Spirit because sin hurts people and the Holy Spirit loves people. Further, when a believer walks in rebellion and willful sin, the Holy Spirit experiences grief because the rebellion creates a sudden loss of connectedness with a person He loves—even though that connection will eventually be restored.

As a believer, you don't lose your salvation when you sin, because your salvation is based on grace through faith. However, when you're in willful rebellion, you do interrupt your fellowship with the Holy Spirit—and that loss of connection with someone He loves produces grief in Him.

God has a mind, a will, and emotions. This means He has a soul. And this is true for God the Father, God the Son, and God the Holy Spirit.

As Christians, we have Someone living within us who is God. He has the mind of God, He knows the will of God, and He knows God's feelings. He resides within us because He wants to help us think the way God thinks, desire what God desires, and feel what God feels. What a privilege!

Week 2

What is This Person Like?

Perhaps the best place to learn about the Holy Spirit begins with Jesus and the words He used to introduce the Spirit to the disciples, as recorded in John 14. Jesus begins with words of comfort: "Don't let your hearts be troubled. I'm going away but I will come back" (paraphrased). Then, in John 14:16, Jesus gets to the core of what He wants these men to understand:

"And I will pray the Father, and He will give you another Helper, that He may abide with you forever—the Spirit of truth, whom the world cannot receive, because it neither sees Him nor knows Him; but you know Him, for He dwells with you and will be in you."

Note the word Helper. The person the Father will send sounds mysterious, but Jesus tells the disciples that the role and nature of this person is to "help." Although Jesus spoke these words to a small group of his closest friends and followers, they are also meant for us. The truth of the Holy Spirit living with and in us assures us that we never have to feel alone.

What kind of "help" will the Holy Spirit provide? Jesus gives part of the answer in John 14:25–26:

"These things I have spoken to you while being present with you. But the Helper, the Holy Spirit, whom the Father will send in My name, He will teach you all things, and bring to your remembrance all things that I said to you."

Here Jesus lists two of the many ways this person will be of help. First, "He will teach you all things." What an incredible promise. There's no subject in which God isn't an expert. He has all the answers. Secondly, He says the Holy Spirit will help us remember His teaching. A little later in this conversation with the disciples, Jesus explains that the Holy Spirit will "testify" of Himself (John 15:26).

In John 16, Jesus gives the disciples His most thorough introduction to the Holy Spirit:

"Nevertheless I tell you the truth. It is to your advantage that I go away; for if I do not go away, the Helper will not come to you; but if I depart, I will send Him to you." (John 16:7)

Jesus is essentially saying, "So wonderful is this one who will be sent that it is a much better thing for you if I go away. Because if I don't go, He can't come!" (paraphrased)

In John 16:12–15, Jesus says:

"I still have many things to say to you, but you cannot bear them now. However, when He, the Spirit of truth, has come, He will guide you into all truth; for He will not speak on His own authority, but whatever He hears He will speak; and He will tell you things to come. He will glorify Me, for He will take of what is Mine and declare it to you."

"All truth." That's quite a benefit of friendship with the Holy Spirit. No wonder Jesus refers to Him as "the Helper."

In each of these four instances, the Greek word translated "Helper" is parakletos. The Greek word appears only five times in the entire New Testament and you've just seen four of them.

When the typical Greek speaker or writer in the First Century used this word, they were talking about a person who pleads your case like a lawyer before a judge, or someone who goes before you to intercede with someone on your behalf. It was also used to describe one who consoles or comforts. (This is why the old King James version translated this word "Comforter." What an amazing way to think of who the Holy Spirit is and how He is our Helper!)

He is also a Friend (and He's not weird!). Not surprisingly, Satan will do anything he can to keep believers from embracing the gift of the Holy Spirit's friendship. One of his primary strategies for keeping people from experiencing all the amazing help and benefits that come from a relationship with the Holy Spirit is to convince us that doing so will make us weird.

Of course, Satan has a lot of help in reinforcing that lie. The world has its share of truly eccentric people. There are weird people in the world, but the Holy Spirit Himself is not weird. He is kind, compassionate and gentle.

And He is God. The promise of the indwelling presence of the Holy Spirit is some of the best news mankind has ever received. People who say they don't want to have anything to do with the Holy Spirit may not realize they are actually saying they don't want to have anything to do with God.

The Holy Spirit isn't strange. He is a wonderful, kind, and sensitive person. And real friendship with Him can change your life. In John 16:8-11, we find Jesus offering additional details about how the Holy Spirit helps us. In fact, He mentions three more key aspects to the Helper's ministry:

"And when He has come, He will convict the world of sin, and of righteousness, and of judgment: of sin, because they do not believe in Me; of righteousness, because I go to My Father and you see Me no more; of judgment, because the ruler of this world is judged."

Jesus names three areas the Holy Spirit will "convict" the world concerning—sin, righteousness and judgment. What does Jesus mean by the word "convict"? Jesus is talking about conviction in the sense of belief or persuasion. Simply put, convict means to convince.

In verse 9, Jesus says the Holy Spirit will convict the world "of sin, because they do not believe in me." We need to understand that when the Holy Spirit convicts lost people of sin—in other words, convinces them that sin is ruling their lives—that's a good thing! This conviction is the only way people become aware that they need the Savior.

The Holy Spirit also convicts us of righteousness. Righteousness means having a "right standing" with God. When Jesus says the Holy Spirit will convict us of righteousness, He is referring to the fact that we all need to be convinced that righteousness exists—and that it's even possible to have a right standing with God. In addition, once we're born again, the Holy Spirit's role is to convince us that we have been made righteous through the blood of Jesus Christ.

Finally, the Holy Spirit was sent to convince the world of "judgment because the ruler of this world is judged" (John 16:11). This is clearly the enemy Jesus is talking about. Satan was the ruler of the world, but he was judged 2,000 years ago through Jesus' sacrifice and subsequent victory over death, hell and the grave. The Holy Spirit convicts us of this truth by convincing us that the former ruler of this world, Satan, has been judged and kicked out. He no longer has any authority in our lives. He's an outlaw.

There are three aspects to the Holy Spirit's personhood and role in our lives. He is our Helper. He is our Friend. And He is God.

Week 3

The Grand Entry

Begin by reading Acts, chapter 2:1–12.

Pentecost was and is one of three major feasts in the nation of Israel. God Himself instituted these events through Moses. The Jewish holy calendar contains a total of seven such feasts, but all seven fall within three major multi-day holidays occurring in the first, third, and seventh months of the Jewish calendar. These three holidays are the Feast of Passover, the Feast of Pentecost, and the Feast of Tabernacles.

As the name suggests, the Feast of Pentecost was always celebrated on the fiftieth day after the Passover festival. *Pente* is the Greek word for "five," and the suffix *koste* indicates "times ten." This feast commemorated God giving the law to Moses on Mt. Sinai fifty days after the exodus from Egypt.

Never was Jerusalem more packed with people and from a more diverse range of nations than during the eight-week period leading up to Passover and running through Pentecost. This is the setting for the events of Pentecost Sunday.

Acts 2 describes how the sound of a hurricane filled the room and a visible manifestation of a tongue of fire rested upon each of the 120 individuals present. This resulted in all of them speaking in "unknown tongues." But what happened next?

People far beyond the walls of the upper room heard the sound of the wind. As a result of the sound, a "multitude came together." Once the huge crowd had gathered, they witnessed something that "confused" them. The multitude was bewildered "because everyone heard them speak in his own language."

Two miracles seem to be at work here. First, 120 people suddenly began speaking in various heavenly languages they'd never before known. Second, thousands of people heard these individuals speaking in their own native languages.

For the eleven remaining disciples of Jesus and 109 others gathered in the room on Pentecost Sunday, the outpouring of the Holy Spirit changed everything.

Before that day, they struggled to understand the Scriptures. Afterward, they realized that the entire Old Testament pointed prophetically and symbolically to the life and redeeming work of Jesus. What had previously been shrouded in mystery suddenly became clear.

Way back at Mt. Sinai God wrote His law, will and truth on tablets of stone. On the day of Pentecost, God, for the very first time in human history, began to write His law, will and truth on the hearts of men and women.

The transformation brought by the outpouring of the Holy Spirit on the day of Pentecost was nothing short of astonishing. That brings us to the next logical questions. Can we experience the miracle of Pentecost Sunday today? And if so, how?

For an answer, back up a step and look at some important words of Jesus in the previous chapter of Acts:

And being assembled together with them, He commanded them not to depart from Jerusalem, but to wait for the Promise of the Father, "which," He said, "you have heard from Me; for John truly baptized with water, but you shall be baptized with the Holy Spirit not many days from now" (Acts 1:4-5).

Notice the word promise in Jesus' statement: "the Promise of the Father." This promise isn't a *what* but a *whom*: "For John truly baptized with water, but you shall be baptized with the Holy Spirit, not many days from now."

Notice that Peter ended his sermon in Acts 2 by referring to "the promise" (v.39). Of course, just ten days earlier, Jesus had also referred to the Holy Spirit as the promise. Now Peter says that the promise belongs "to you, and to your children and all who are afar off and as many as the Lord our God will call."

Peter makes it clear that the promise of the Holy Spirit belongs not only to the people he's directly speaking to. The promise applies to future generations, too ("your children"). And the phrase "all who are afar off" refers directly to you.

You can experience Pentecost. The promise belongs to anyone who God calls—in any place and in any time.

To explore the reasons why we can experience Pentecost now, return to Acts 2:3–4:

*Then there appeared to them divided tongues, as of fire, and one sat upon **each** of them. And they were **all** filled with the Holy Spirit and began to speak with other tongues, as the Spirit gave them utterance.*

The words each and all in these verses are emphasized because these words tell us something important about what happened on that day. The 120 individuals in that room represented a wide spectrum of society. Rich and influential people like Joseph of Arimathea and Nicodemus were probably there. In addition, the formerly blind beggars and lepers whom Jesus had healed and former prostitutes he ministered to were surely there too. Some, like the eleven disciples, were in "full-time ministry." Others were simple merchants, farmers, or homemakers.

In other words, this baptism of the Spirit of God wasn't only for the elite or those in full-time ministry. They were "all filled with the Holy Spirit" and they all "began to speak with other tongues as the Spirit gave them utterance."

The baptism of the Holy Spirit is for everyone.

Week 4

The Power Transfer

The sixth chapter of Hebrews begins with an exhortation to believers to grow up and move on from "elementary" or "foundational" doctrines. Among the "foundational" things mentioned in that passage is "the doctrine of baptisms." (Notice that the word baptisms is plural.)

That there is more than one type or kind of baptism is a foundational truth. Nevertheless, there is much confusion surrounding the connection between baptism and the Holy Spirit. It comes in part because the Bible mentions several different baptisms and two of them involve the Holy Spirit.

Most of us are familiar with "water baptism." We can easily understand this baptism because the Bible depicts it clearly— take John the Baptist's activity in the Jordan River, for example. And if you attend a church that practices it, you see it with your own eyes all the time.

Still, the Bible mentions two baptisms that you can't see with your physical eyes. You can only see the aftereffects of them in a person's life. Let's explore all three to understand the differences.

The first of the baptisms a person can and should experience is mentioned in 1 Corinthians 12:13:

"For by one Spirit we were all baptized into one body— whether Jews or Greeks, whether slaves or free."

Note the grammar in this verse. Do you see the preposition by at the beginning of the verse? The dictionary tells us that by: "identifies an agent performing an action." In other words, by refers to who is doing the baptizing.

So, who is doing the baptizing in this verse? It's the Holy Spirit. When you experienced salvation, you were baptized into a body—the Body of Christ. The Holy Spirit is the agent who did the baptizing. This is a baptism of/by the Holy Spirit. But it's not a baptism in the Holy Spirit.

The way you became a "member" of the Body of Christ is by the Holy Spirit "baptizing" you into it. Then, if we are obedient to the commands of scripture, we choose to experience a second baptism, this one in water, which is an outward sign of what has happened inwardly.

The best-known baptizer in Scripture was John the Baptist. In Matthew 3:11, he mentions a type of baptism other than water, saying:

"I indeed baptize you with water unto repentance, but He who is coming after me is mightier than I, whose sandals I am not worthy to carry. He will baptize you with the Holy Spirit and fire."

John is talking about Jesus. To paraphrase John's statement: "You've seen me immersing repentant people in water, but I am just a forerunner for the much greater one, Jesus, who will immerse reborn people in the fire of the Holy Spirit."

John's declaration is one of just a handful of statements or events that appear in all four gospels—Matthew, Mark, Luke, and John. Who is doing the baptizing in this verse? It's Jesus!

What is He baptizing us in or with? The Holy Spirit! In other words, only Jesus performs this baptism, immersing us in the Holy Spirit. Scripture tells us this four times in four separate gospels.

To compare, look back at that baptism of salvation described in 1 Corinthians 12:13: "For by one Spirit we were all baptized into one body—whether Jews or Greeks, whether slaves or free." The baptizer in this case is the Holy Spirit, baptizing us into Jesus.

In the gospels, we see the reverse. Beyond the baptism into Jesus (the New Birth) and water baptism, Scripture repeatedly describes this third baptism where Jesus baptizes us into the Holy Spirit. Jesus even commanded His disciples to wait in Jerusalem until they received it.

Jesus' final word of instruction to his followers was not "go." It was "wait." We find this command recorded in the final chapter of Luke. Jesus appears to His disciples and gives them some words of explanation and instruction. When He finishes speaking, they see Him taken up into the heavens. Right before that moment He says:

"Behold, I send the Promise of My Father upon you; but tarry in the city of Jerusalem until you are endued with power from on high" (Luke 24:49).

The word "tarry" simply means "wait." Don't you think Jesus would very carefully choose the words He knew would be the last the disciples would hear Him speak? You would assume these were important instructions.

His final instructions were "wait." Wait for what? The "promise." As we learned earlier, Jesus' last words are also recorded in the first chapter of Acts:

*And being assembled together with them, He commanded them not to depart from Jerusalem, but to **wait** for the Promise of the Father, "which," He said, "you have heard from Me; for John truly baptized with water, but you shall be baptized with the Holy Spirit not many days from now"* (Acts 1:4–5, emphasis added).

We previously saw that each of the four gospels record a promise that Jesus will baptize His followers in the Holy Spirit. This represents a fifth mention of baptism in the Holy Spirit.

Jesus told His disciples to "wait" rather than "go" change the world. He knew that if they went without the empowerment of the Holy Spirit, nothing would happen. He is telling them: "Don't leave this place until you've received what I've promised you—a Helper."

If you've been born again, the Holy Spirit baptized you into Jesus at the moment you were saved and you are bound for heaven. To go to heaven, you need only to be saved. But to live a victorious Christian life, you need to be water baptized and Spirit baptized. Have you asked Jesus to baptize you into the Holy Spirit?

Three baptisms appear throughout the Bible. For example, 1 John 5:7 says: "There are three that bear witness in heaven. The Father, the Word and the Holy Spirit; and these three are one. And there are three that bear witness on earth: the Spirit, the water, and the blood; and these three agree as one."

Spirit. Water. Blood. This verse says that these three all "bear witness on earth" just as the Father, Son and Spirit all "bear witness in heaven."

Here are the three baptisms in reverse order! The three "witnesses" on earth are the Holy Spirit baptism, water baptism, and salvation through the blood of Jesus Christ.

These three "witnesses" can be summarized this way: When you are saved, you became a new person. When you are baptized in water, the old person is cut off. And when you are baptized in the Holy Spirit, you received the power to walk in the new.

Week 5

Power for Living a Supernatural Life

Jesus sent the Holy Spirit so we could be "helped" with supernatural power for victorious living. The key to receiving this kind of help lies in understanding the role of three distinct baptisms.

You've already discovered numerous New Testament examples of the principle of three baptisms. However, if this is a valid biblical truth (and it is) we should also be able to find some examples of Old Testament foreshadowing and symbolism of the same principle.

We can start with Abraham. Genesis 12:1 begins Abraham's story by telling us:

Now the LORD had said to Abram: "Get out of your country, from your family, and from your father's house, to a land that I will show you."

This call for Abram to leave his native country is a salvation-like experience. When we are saved, we leave the kingdom where we were born and become citizens of a new kingdom. (See Colossians 1:13.)

We find the next big milestone in Abram's life in Genesis 15:17–18. This describes a "covenant cutting" ceremony between God and Abram. This event is a type of water baptism—which represents a cutting away of our fleshly desires.

In ancient times, two parties entered into sacred covenant by sacrificing an animal, cutting it in half, and then placing the two halves on the ground with space between the halves. The two parties walked between the halves as a part of swearing an unbreakable life-and-death oath of faithfulness. The act symbolized that the two parties were in covenant by blood.

This symbolizes baptism because the parties had to "pass through" the pieces that represented death. The sacrificed animal signified that if either party violated the covenant, they would die. In the same way, passing through the waters of baptism signifies a type of death to the old self.

Another Old Testament event illuminates this idea more deeply. The children of Israel departed Egypt because the blood of a lamb on the doorposts of their homes caused the angel of Death to pass over their houses. Just like Abraham, they "went out" of the pagan country they'd called home for more than 400 years and headed toward a land of promise and blessing. In other words, the leaving of Egypt symbolizes salvation.

What happened immediately after that? The Israelites found themselves backed up against the Red Sea with Pharaoh's chariots bearing down on them. Moses used his staff to part the sea, and the Israelites "passed through" the waters that had suddenly been cut in half. They walked between the two halves of water to safety. When Pharaoh's army entered the sea, however, the halves came back together and drowned them all—cutting off the flesh of the old life the Israelites were leaving behind!

Jump back to Abraham's story to see an event that symbolizes Holy Spirit baptism. Genesis 17:5 states: *"No longer shall your name be called Abram, but your name shall be called Abraham; for I have made you a father of many nations."* You might be wondering, "What does a simple name change have to do with Holy Spirit baptism?"

The answer is beautifully simple. The change from Abram to Abraham required putting the "ha" sound in the middle. There are no consonants in written Hebrew, so in the original language, God added the equivalent of the Hebrew letter "H." In Hebrew, this letter is also the word *ruah*, which represents *spirit, breath,* and *wind.* Think about how you have to breathe out and create wind to make the sound: "ha."

This word appears many times in the Old Testament. With Abram, God literally opens up Abram's name and pours *ruah*—His own Spirit—into it. And it becomes Abra-*ha*-m!

Is it stretching things to think that these Old Testament events are symbolic of baptism? Take note of these words from the Apostle Paul:

"Moreover, brethren, I do not want you to be unaware that all our fathers were under the cloud, all passed through the sea, all were baptized into Moses in the cloud and in the sea" (1 Corinthians 10:1–2).

Paul points out that the children of Israel symbolically experienced all three baptisms. They were "baptized into Moses in the cloud and in the sea."

The tabernacle of Moses provides another example of this symbolism. The tabernacle was the portable tent complex that God instructed Moses and the Israelites to construct as they wandered in the wilderness. He provided incredibly detailed instructions about how they were to build, lay out, and furnish the structure.

The tabernacle had an Outer Court; an interior space called the Holy Place; and then a smaller space within that called the Most Holy Place or "The Holy of Holies." The Ark of the Covenant was kept in the Holy of Holies, and this was the place of God's manifested presence. No one could simply enter the Most Holy Place off the street.

Coming into the presence of God as a sinful and fallen person would be fatal. The sheer glory and purity of God would kill anyone who tried. According to the strict instructions God gave Moses, Aaron, and the Levitical priests, a high priest needed to go through three stations or tasks before he could enter the Holy of Holies.

First, the priest had to sacrifice a spotless, unblemished lamb on the altar. Next, the priest went to a basin filled with water, called a laver, where he washed and made himself ceremonially clean. Finally, the priest went to a place where he was anointed with oil. Only then could the priest approach the presence of God in the Holy of Holies.

The blood of the spotless lamb is a reference to salvation through the blood of Jesus. The washing with water at the laver represents water baptism. And oil has always been a symbol for the Holy Spirit in Scripture. The pouring of anointing oil over the head of the priest is an amazing picture of the anointing upon a believer being baptized in the Holy Spirit.

On the Day of Pentecost, Peter stood up and delivered the first Holy Spirit-inspired prophetic sermon. Without preparation, he cites Old Testament passages that spoke of the outpouring of the Holy Spirit and how His coming would empower God's people to prophesy. The formerly timid Peter finishes by boldly proclaiming Jesus as the Messiah.

In support of Peter's preaching, the Holy Spirit did what He was specifically sent to do: He convicted hearts and drew people to Jesus. Notice how the people listening to Peter responded:

*Now when they heard **this**, they were cut to the heart, and said to Peter and the rest of the apostles, "Men **and** brethren, what shall we do?" (Acts 2:37).*

Of course, Peter happily answers their question:

Then Peter said to them, "Repent, and let every one of you be baptized in the name of Jesus Christ for the remission of sins; and you shall receive the gift of the Holy Spirit. For the promise is to you and to your children, and to all who are afar off, as many as the Lord our God will call" (Acts 2:38–39).

Peter quickly outlined three simple steps:

1. Repent

2. Be water baptized

3. Receive the Holy Spirit

What Peter outlines here goes two steps beyond simply receiving salvation (as wonderful and vital as that is). He presents a roadmap for experiencing every amazing thing that is available to the believer in Christ.

Week 6

The Bringer of Gifts

When you come across the word "gift" in the New Testament, it is almost always a translation of the Greek word *charisma*. Or when it is translated "gifts" it is the plural form *charismata*. It's the root of our English word, "charismatic."

Even in the Body of Christ, many people are confused and ignorant about spiritual gifts. The use of the word *ignorant* here isn't meant to sound unkind—it simply refers to a lack of accurate information. It is just that many people operate without a solid understanding of what the Bible teaches about this vitally important subject.

Paul begins 1 Corinthians 12 with the words, "Now concerning spiritual gifts, brethren, I do not want you to be ignorant." Apparently, a lot of confusion and ignorance about spiritual gifts also existed 2,000 years ago.

Obviously, the believers within the church had experienced some confusion about how spiritual gifts work and how they should be utilized within the church—particularly during public worship services. With the above phrase, Paul begins a section of instruction and explanation that continues for three chapters.

Let's look at the first of these verses and then break them down for additional insight:

There are diversities of gifts, but the same Spirit. There are differences of ministries, but the same Lord. And there are diversities of activities, but it is the same God who works all in all (1 Corinthians 12:4-6).

The Greek word translated "ministries" in the verse above is one that refers to "a place of service. And the Greek word translated "activities" is *energema*, which means "the thing that is produced" or "the outcome." *Energema* is also the Greek root of our English word *energy*. Paul is teaching that there is a place of service in the Body of Christ for every believer; and we are energized by God when we use the gifts of grace from the Holy Spirit in that place of service.

What kind of outcomes will this process produce? Paul tells us in the very next verse: *But the manifestation of the Spirit is given to each one for the profit of all* (1 Corinthians 12:7).

Why does the Holy Spirit give spiritual gifts to us? So those gifts can be released in "ministries," "for the profit of all." He gives us gifts so we can be a blessing to others. Notice also that these gifts are given to "each one." Not some. Not most. "Each one" of us is the recipient of these spiritual gifts in various times and places if we are born again and are willing to be used by God to bring about "the profit of all."

All of this prompts an important question: "What kinds of gifts?" What do these gifts look like? In the next few verses, Paul lists nine of them:

For to one is given the word of wisdom through the Spirit, to another the word of knowledge through the same Spirit, to another faith by the same Spirit, to another gifts of healings by the same Spirit, to another the working of miracles, to another prophecy, to another discerning of spirits, to another different kinds of tongues, to another the interpretation of tongues.

But one and the same Spirit works all these things, distributing to each one individually as He wills.
(1 Corinthians 12:8–11).

At the front end of that list we find: "For to one is given the word of wisdom through the Spirit, to another the word of knowledge through the same Spirit" (1 Corinthians 12:8). Take note of the "word of wisdom" and the "word of knowledge." We can classify these two gifts of the Spirit under the general heading "Discerning Gifts." Another appropriate label would be "Perceiving Gifts."

Either name fits because when these gifts operate, you are empowered to discern or perceive certain truths that can help another person.

What do these gifts look like in operation? A word of knowledge is the Holy Spirit allowing you to know something specific that you didn't learn by natural means. It's a supernatural impartation of information you couldn't possibly know through natural processes.

Jesus operated in this gift all the time. (Remember, Jesus is fully God and fully man, but while He was on earth He depended on the power of the Holy Spirit to work through Him just like we do.) Do you recall His encounter with the Samaritan woman at the well? She told Jesus that she wasn't married, and He responded by saying, "You have well said, 'I have no husband,' for you have had five husbands, and the one whom you now have is not your husband; in that you spoke truly" (John 4:17–18).

That was a pretty specific piece of information Jesus knew about a perfect stranger. The Holy Spirit didn't reveal the Samaritan woman's secret to Jesus to embarrass her. He spoke it to open her eyes because God loved her and wanted her to be free and whole. Gifts of the Spirit are always given to edify, to encourage, and to set captive people free.

Another gift on the list of nine found in 1 Corinthians 12:8–11 that falls under the category of Discerning Gifts is what the Bible calls "discerning of spirits."

Discerning of spirits involves the Holy Spirit making a believer aware of the presence of a demonic spirit. It is a gift bestowed by and through the Holy Spirit. The apostle Paul operated in this gift in Acts 16 where a demonized young girl had been following them around crying out and creating a distraction.

After putting up with her for several days, he finally got fed up and cast the demon out of her. But he only knew a demon was present to be cast out because a gift of discerning of spirits revealed it to him.

Another one of the Discerning Gifts is "the word of wisdom." This gift of the Holy Spirit is simply a divine answer or solution for a particular question or challenge.

Sometimes the word of wisdom comes in knowing exactly the right thing to say. Again, Jesus operated in this gift all the time. When confronted by a group of skeptics who were sure they were going to trip up Jesus with a trick question, He would turn the tables on them every time.

At other times, this gift results in knowing exactly the right thing to do. When Jesus and Peter were about to be late in paying the temple tax, Jesus got a word of wisdom that solved the problem for both of them: "Go to the sea, cast in a hook, and take the fish that comes up first. And when you have opened its mouth, you will find a piece of money; take that and give it to them for Me and you." Peter obeyed. Problem solved. (Matthew 17:27)

Paul was also a recipient of this gift on numerous occasions. In Acts 27, we find him as a prisoner of the Roman government on a ship headed for Rome. The ship ends up in a terrible storm and is about to sink. The hired crew of the ship is about to sneak off in the only lifeboat, which would leave Paul, his fellow prisoners, and their Roman guards behind. At the critical moment, as everyone else is panicking and paralyzed with fear, Paul knows just what to do. He tells the Roman guards the actions that will save them all. The guards listen to him, and all were saved just as Paul promised.

The word of wisdom, the word of knowledge, and the discerning of spirits—these are the Discerning Gifts. They are awesome, but the Holy Spirit has much, much more in His arsenal of blessing and empowerment.

Week 7

More Gifts

As we explored in the previous session, the Discerning Gifts involve a supernatural impartation of information to the mind. They allow you to know something you didn't learn by natural means. On the other hand, the Declarative Gifts each involve a form of declaration of divine truth or supernatural message.

Let's take a fresh look at that section of Paul's list. He says the Holy Spirit gives ". . . to another prophecy . . . to another different kinds of tongues, to another the interpretation of tongues" (1 Corinthians 12:10). Here we have three unique and wonderful gifts—prophecy, various tongues, and interpretation of tongues. Let's take a brief look at each.

When the Bible speaks of a word of prophecy it simply means "a message of encouragement from God, delivered through a human vessel, to another person or persons."

Please notice three elements in that definition. First, a word of prophecy is a message of *encouragement*— not discouragement, not correction or rebuke, and not judgment. In 1 Corinthians 14:3, Paul provides the threefold role of prophecy: *"But he who prophesies speaks edification and exhortation and comfort to men."* A great way to test the validity of a prophetic word is to ask; did that word of prophecy bring edification, exhortation, or comfort to the hearer?

God is an encourager. And 1 Corinthians 14:31 reveals that "all can prophesy." So, when you allow God to speak through you, you are likely to speak words of encouragement. When you have spoken words of encouragement, exhortation or comfort in the past, you may very well have been prophesying without knowing it!

That brings us to the next of the Declarative Gifts, the gift of tongues. The gift of tongues is a message from God to others in a language unknown to the person through whom the message comes. There is a difference between the "gift of tongues," which the Holy Spirit bestows on certain occasions distributing it "as He wills," and the "prayer language" that every believer receives when they are baptized in the Holy Spirit.

This takes us to the third of the Declarative Gifts—interpretation of tongues. A biblical definition of this gift would be: "understanding and expressing the thought or intent of a message in tongues." The key words in that definition are *thought or intent*.

When you receive the gift of interpretation of tongues, you get a supernatural understanding of the general gist of the message being communicated. This explains why the gift is called *interpretation* of tongues rather than *translation* of tongues.

The next group of gifts are often labeled the "Dynamic Gifts" because they tend to display the power of God. Going back to our list of the nine gifts of the Holy Spirit listed by Paul in 1 Corinthians 12, we find:

"But the manifestation of the Spirit is given to each one for the profit of all . . . to another faith by the same Spirit, to

another gifts of healings by the same Spirit, to another the working of miracles" (1 Corinthians 12:7–10).

Once again, we have three distinct gifts in this grouping—faith, gifts of healings, and working of miracles. While these are three distinct gifts, they can produce similar results.

First, there is the gift of faith. Paul is talking about an impartation of something distinct from the everyday faith we are called to exercise in our Christian walk. That's why some people refer to this as the "gift of special faith." The gift of faith can be defined as "a supernatural impartation of belief and confidence for a specific situation."

Countless Christians can testify that in a moment of severe crisis or in a time of great need, they suddenly found themselves infused with a supernatural level of faith that everything would be okay. The faith they experienced in that moment was significantly higher and stronger than the faith they walk in day to day.

The Holy Spirit also imparts what Paul calls "gifts of healings." These are "supernatural endowments of divine health."

This is not the Holy Spirit depositing a special gifting in special people so they have the power to pray for people and see them healed. The Lord may indeed use a particular person consistently in the area of healing, but it is the Holy Spirit who owns the gift and distributes it individually moment-by-moment, as He wills.

Your neighbor in your small group Bible study is just as likely to be used by the Holy Spirit to deliver God's healing power to you as the most famous minister. However, this gift doesn't have to come through another person at all. Countless people have been miraculously healed in their prayer closets when all alone.

In the same way, the gift called "the working of miracles" isn't deposited in just a special few people who carry it for the rest of their lives. The power to see a miracle take place is available to all believers, and the Holy Spirit distributes this gift as He wills in momentary situations.

We can define the gift of the working of miracles as "divine intervention that alters circumstances." Is this something you'd like to experience? Would you be blessed if, from time to time, the miraculous power of God turned around a negative situation?

God is still working miracles. God is immutable—meaning He never changes. He's the same yesterday, today, and forever. He worked miracles in the days of the Old Testament, in the days of the New Testament, and He still works miracles today.

An intimate, personal relationship with the Holy Spirit is available to every believer. At the Last Supper, Jesus, in so many words, told His disciples to say "goodbye" to Him so they could prepare to say "hello" to the Holy Spirit (John 14:15–16). There is great joy and blessing that comes from saying "hello" to the Helper Jesus sent.

Week 8

The Language of Heaven

One of the great tragedies of the last 100 years of Church history has been the way Satan, the enemy of the Church, has successfully made the gift of prayer language (praying/worshipping in tongues) so controversial and successfully made huge segments of the Body of Christ reluctant to embrace *any* of the empowerments of the Holy Spirit.

Back in 1904 there was a great revival in the nation of Wales. It has since come to be known, appropriately enough, as The Welsh Revival. In this remarkable move of God lukewarm Christians suddenly caught fire for God, churches filled, bars and houses of prostitution closed for lack of business and, most importantly, more than 100,000 people were born again. It all began with some dedicated people praying for an outpouring of the Holy Spirit. And throughout all of it, extraordinary manifestations similar to those recorded in the book of Acts were reported.

Like seeds that blow in the wind and take root far away from the original plant, that spirit of revival crossed the Atlantic and sprang up in several places in the United States—particularly among a little group of dedicated prayer warriors meeting in a house on Bonnie Brae Avenue near downtown Los Angeles in 1906. The people there had been praying for God to move in power in America as He had moved in Wales.

Soon these people of prayer began to experience the book of Acts in their gatherings—particularly various people speaking in tongues and prophesying. The numbers in attendance swelled and eventually the meetings were moved to an abandoned Methodist church a few blocks away on Azusa Street. Soon thousands were coming and being touched by God in remarkable ways.

The outpouring there came to be known as the Azusa Street Revival; and it is no exaggeration to say that it changed the course of Christianity in America and throughout the world. Many individuals who came from across the country to the Azusa Street meetings experienced the baptism in the Holy Spirit and took that spark back to their home churches.

Many believers who experienced this very beneficial release of the Holy Spirit in their lives found themselves criticized and ostracized for it. There were many well-meaning Christians who didn't see that God was behind this and that the fruit it was producing in the lives of others was good.

Of course, no Christian is immune from the temptation to turn something that has the life and breath of God on it into lifeless religion. And within a generation, religion began to seep into some aspects of the Pentecostal movement. Some who had been offended by the persecution they received because of the gift of speaking in tongues, elevated tongues to a place the Holy Spirit never intended it to have in our theology. The result was a rigid obsession with "the initial evidence of speaking in tongues" as being the only valid indicator of Holy Spirit baptism.

As a result, many started putting pressure on people to produce the "evidence" that they had achieved this special spiritual plateau. For many, tongues became a demand rather than a desire. For others it became an award proudly achieved rather than a gift humbly received. This wrongly moved the focus to the gift rather than the Gift Giver—God the Holy Spirit.

Return to the now-familiar words of 1 Corinthians 14:

For he who speaks in a tongue does not speak to men but to God, for no one understands him; however, in the spirit he speaks mysteries (1 Corinthians 14:2, emphasis added).

Please take note of the phrase, ". . . in the spirit" in the verse above. It's a significant set of words because Paul will use them several times throughout this chapter, as will other New Testament writers.

In 1 Corinthians 14:2, Paul gives us several key pieces of information. Yes, he tells us that speaking in tongues is speaking mysteries, or hidden things, "in the spirit." But before that he tells us that a person who speaks in tongues isn't speaking to people (in this natural realm). He is speaking to God (in the spiritual realm).

Now what is a common term we use to describe "speaking to God?" *Prayer*! Prayer is simply speaking to God. And anyone who speaks to God is praying. That's pretty elementary. It also explains why Paul is telling the Corinthian church that their public worship services aren't the place for exercising this gift.

If a person stands up and delivers a long prayer in tongues, no one but the person praying is helped. But if the same person stands up and delivers prophetic encouragement in the native language of everyone gathered, then everyone walks away encouraged.

Look, for example at 1 Corinthians 14:14 where Paul says, "For if I pray in a tongue, my spirit prays, but my understanding is unfruitful."

There are three packets of powerful spiritual truth in that little verse. Let's break it down:

1. If I *pray* in a tongue,

2. my *spirit* prays,

3. but my *understanding* (mind) is unfruitful.

This confirms that we can indeed "pray" in tongues, which is why it is so often referred to as a prayer language.

Notice also that when you pray in an unknown tongue, it is your "spirit" which prays. You will recall that early in our journey we learned that we are all three-part beings. We are each comprised of spirit, soul and body. More specifically, you *are* a spirit, you *have* a soul, and you *live* in a body.

Paul follows this verse by posing a rhetorical question: "What is the conclusion then?" He essentially says, "So what is the logical thing to do based upon this information?" He then answers his own question:

"I will pray with the spirit, and I will also pray with the understanding. I will sing with the spirit, and I will also sing with the understanding." (1 Corinthians 14:15)

Praying "with the spirit" clearly refers to praying in tongues, because in the preceding verse Paul said, "If I pray in a tongue, my spirit prays, but my understanding is unfruitful."

Here God's Word is giving us instruction on having a balanced prayer and devotional life. Pray with the spirit *and* pray with the understanding. In your times of private worship, sing with the spirit *and* sing with the understanding.

Receiving and using prayer language is scriptural. In fact, Paul bluntly said, "I wish you all spoke with tongues" (1 Corinthians 14:5). But the gift is more than biblical, it is also a benefit!

Examine 1 Corinthians 14:4 to identify one of the key benefits of praying in the spirit. You will recall that Paul wrote: "He who speaks in a tongue edifies himself, but he who prophesies edifies the church."

Edify means "to build up, strengthen or improve." In other words, when you pray in tongues you are strengthening yourself spiritually. And when you publicly deliver a word from the Lord in a language everyone understands, you are strengthening the church spiritually.

When you pray in tongues, or in the spirit, you build *yourself* up. And being built up is vital if we're going to be useful, productive, victorious citizens in God's kingdom. It is also true that in a public worship gathering, your focus should be on building up the Body as a whole. In reality, we're not much help to others unless we've first built ourselves up. If we don't obtain some spiritual supply in the prayer closet, we don't have much to give when we encounter hurting or discouraged people.

Yes, the gift of prayer language is scriptural and also a great benefit. But it is also a *choice*. In other words, you have complete control over whether or not you express this gift (or any of the Holy Spirit's gifts, for that matter).

One of the most prevalent misconceptions is the fear that once you're open to receiving your prayer language, it will somehow just involuntarily come pouring out of you. Because of this misconception many people who might otherwise be open to receiving the grace of a prayer language are fearful of it because they don't want to be in the check out line at the grocery store and suddenly start uncontrollably delivering a message in tongues.

Nothing about the gifts of the Holy Spirit work that way. The fact is, operating in any of the spiritual gifts is a choice you make. Recall Paul's simple summing up of all he'd written about tongues in 1 Corinthians 14. He said:

What is the conclusion then? I will pray with the spirit, and I will also pray with the understanding. I will sing with the spirit, and I will also sing with the understanding (1 Corinthians 14:15).

Notice the four appearances of the word "will" in the verse above. This makes it clear that you have to exercise your will to pray or sing in the spirit just as you do when you pray or sing with your understanding.

You also have to step out in faith. Some say, "If God wants me to have that gift He'll just give it to me." He has! All of His gifts are available to you, but in the same way that a person with the "gift of giving" must still step out in faith and write a check, we must choose to step out by an act of our wills.

The gift of prayer language is biblical, beneficial and always a choice.

Leader's Guide

The *The God I Never Knew* Leader's Guide is designed to help you better lead your small group or class through *The God I Never Knew* curriculum. Use this guide along with the curriculum for a life-changing, interactive experience.

Before You Meet

- Ask God to prepare the hearts and minds of the people in your group. Ask Him to show you how to encourage each person to integrate the principles you discover into their daily lives through group discussion and personal journaling.

- Preview the DVD segment for the week.

- Plan how much time you'll allot to each portion of your meeting (see suggested schedule below). In case you're unable to get through them all in the time you have planned, here is a list of the most important questions (from the TALK section) for each week (these questions are also highlighted in the Participant Guide with this color):

SESSION ONE

- Q: If you grew up in church, how was the topic of the Holy Spirit handled where you attended? If you didn't attend church, what was your conception of the Holy Spirit (or "Holy Ghost" in some circles)?

- Q: Read Galatians 5:22–23. What does this list of the "fruits of the Spirit" reveal to you about the Holy Spirit's personality and temperament? How does this picture compare with the way you have perceived the Holy Spirit in the past?

SESSION TWO

- Q: The name "Helper" is translated from the Greek word *parakletos* meaning comforter, intercessor, consoler, and advocate. Which of these descriptions of the Holy Spirit's work has the most significance to you personally? Why?

- Q: Have you ever experienced supernatural "help" that you knew came from The Helper—the Holy Spirit? Describe your experience.

SESSION THREE

- Q: The giving of the Holy Spirit was a supernaturally unifying event. Is there an area of your life—family, work, or school—in which greater unity is needed? How might the fruit or power of the Holy Spirit make a difference in this situation?

- Q: It's easy to see the evidence of the Holy Spirit's presence in the lives of others, but we're often blind to His work and power in ourselves. Point out some ways you have observed the Holy Spirit's activity in the life of another person in the group. (If you don't know any other group members well, talk about the evidence of His work in another person you know.)

SESSION FOUR

- Q: Were you ever baptized in water? If so, what was your understanding of what it meant and what, if anything, was taking place spiritually?

- Q: Jesus instructed his followers to stay in Jerusalem and "wait for the Promise of the Father" (meaning the Holy Spirit). How good are you at *waiting*? Describe a time in which you've experienced a season of waiting for a promise of God.

SESSION FIVE

- Q: Acts 8 and Acts 19 tell of believers who were recently saved and water baptized being invited by Jesus' disciples to receive the Holy Spirit as well. At any point in your Christian life, have you had the sense that you were "missing something?" Why? Describe that feeling.

- Q: God changed the names of Abram and Sarai after He entered into covenant with them. In changing Sarai to Sarah, God "took the 'I' out and put the Spirit in." In what area of your life would it be good to have less "I" and more Holy Spirit?

SESSION SIX

- Q: 1 Corinthians 12:7 says, "But the manifestation of the Spirit is given to each one for the profit of all." In what ways have you been aware of the Holy Spirit working through you to the profit of those around you?

- Q: A word of knowledge is "to know something specific without having learned it by natural means." Have you ever received a word of knowledge from another believer? If you are comfortable talking about it, describe the experience.

SESSION SEVEN

- Q: Have you felt that God wanted you to tell someone something, but you didn't do it? What kept you from speaking out?

- Q: In practical terms, what do you think it means to say "hello" to the Holy Spirit?

SESSION EIGHT

- Q: Have you ever witnessed what you would describe as a true "revival" or a "move of God?" Describe it.

- Q: Romans 8:26 says, "Likewise the Spirit also helps in our weaknesses. For we do not know what we should pray for as we ought, but the Spirit Himself makes intercession for us with groanings which cannot be uttered." (NKJV) Have you ever faced a problem so mystifying that you didn't even know how to begin praying about it? What did you do? How did you pray?

Remember, the goal is not necessarily to get through all of the questions. The highest priority is for the group to learn and engage in dynamic discussion.

Suggested Schedule for the Group

1. RECAP and ENGAGE (5 minutes)

2. WATCH or READ (20 minutes)

3. TALK (35–40 minutes)

4. PRAY (10 minutes)

CPSIA information can be obtained
at www.ICGtesting.com
Printed in the USA
LVOW01s2333151215
466755LV00001B/1/P

9 780989 516730